Would You Rather

for Teens

Quinn Addison

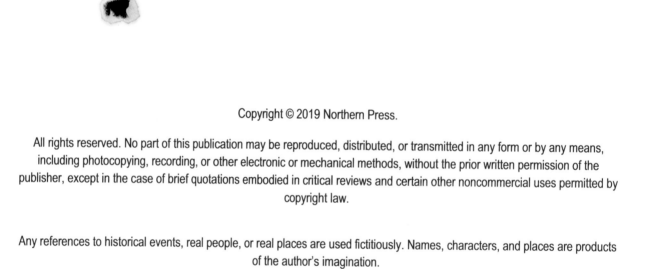

Would you rather be gossiped about or never talked about at all?

Would you rather give up the internet or your pet?

Would you rather be forced to hang out with someone you don't like, or have your brother or sister follow you around school for 1 week straight?

Would you rather publish your diary or make a movie of your most embarrassing moment?

Would you rather count how many spoonful's of water there are in a pool or grains of sand inside a sandbox?

Would you rather go without YouTube the rest of your life or junk food?

Would you rather always wear gloves or ear plugs?

Would you rather be called out by a teacher in school for giving the wrong answer or trip in front of your whole class?

Would you rather have to say everything you think or never say anything at all?

Would you rather have invisibility as a superpower or flying?

Would you rather only be able to shout everything you say or whisper?

Would you rather live in a house that is always too bright or too dark?

Would you rather go surfing in waters where sharks usually linger or go hand-gliding over a forest fire?

Would you rather sing every word you speak or only speak in rhymes?

Would you rather live in a house that's too hot or too cold?

Would you rather be the smartest person in your school or the most popular?

Would you rather have bright red teeth or bright red hair?

Would you rather have the same song stuck in your head constantly or have the same dream every night?

Would you rather have a really nice teacher and learn nothing or have a really hard teacher and learn a lot?

Would you rather live in a desert for a year or in the international space station?

Would you rather be able to control the weather or talk to animals?

Would you rather go 100 years into the future or 200 years into the past?

Would you rather be 20 minutes early to everything or 10 minutes late?

Would you rather have a 3rd leg or a 3rd arm?

Would you rather be super-fast or super strong?

Would you rather go skydiving or climb a mountain?

Would you rather have to wear a winter jacket in the Sahara desert or swim wear in the arctic snow lands?

Would you rather be able to speak every language in the world or know the answer to every trivia question?

Would you rather be a famous movie celebrity or singer celebrity?

Would you rather be captain of the football team or the debate team?

Would you rather be 4 feet tall or 10 feet tall?

Would you rather a raw onion or a whole lemon?

Would you rather be covered in poison ivy or mosquito bites?

Would you rather only eat chicken nuggets for a whole month or pizza?

Would you rather eat a pound of raw tomatoes or broccoli?

Would you rather have hair down to your ankles or be totally bald?

Would you rather go to school with your pants on backwards or your shoes on the wrong feet?

Would you rather have a magic button that made your teacher stop speaking or your best friend?

Would you rather swim in a pool of Hawaiian punch or coca cola?

Would you rather eat an entire birthday cake or a gallon of ice cream?

Would you rather have to ride on the back of a bull or camel?

Would you rather have a family of 9 or have no family at all?

Would you rather spend 1 year as a cop or a teacher?

Would you rather get to change your eye color or hair color?

Would you rather never mentally age or physically?

Would you rather be known for your smarts or your good looks?

Would you rather live forever as a monk or be constantly followed by paparazzi?

Would you rather be debt free forever or guaranteed perfect health forever?

Would you rather be given a lifetime supply of gas for your car or books?

Would you rather be able to cook like a professional chef or act like a pro actor?

Would you rather have an arranged marriage or be single your whole life?

Would you rather be locked in a library or a haunted house for 1 week?

Would you rather be stuck on a bus or on a train?

Would you rather be the lead role in a romance movie or an action thriller movie?

Would you rather spend a 3 week vacation in the Bahamas or all across Europe?

Would you rather give up brushing your teeth forever or brushing your hair?

Would you rather end hunger or racism?

Would you rather own your own cottage with a boat near a lake or your own airplane?

Would you rather have to sing a song in front of strangers or all your friends?

Would you rather be super rich but live 200 years ago or live just below average in today's time?

Would you rather have the best house in a bad neighborhood or the worst house in the best neighborhood?

Would you rather have your first child when you are 18 or 45?

Would you rather date someone you met online or go on a blind date?

Would you rather a bunch of good friend or just 1 best friend?

Would you rather watch the big game at home with all your friends or with just 1 friend live at the stadium?

Would you rather be your own boss or work for someone else?

Would you rather hear the good news first or the bad news?

Would you rather be prosed to (or propose) in public or in front of family?

Would you rather live in a condo in a busy city or on top of a mountain?

Would you rather have a desk job or an outdoor job?

Would you rather get rich through winning the lottery or through hard work?

Would you rather call your crush or text?

Would you rather be stranded on an island with someone you don't like or alone?

Would you rather never eat junk forever or drink 1 cup of pee once?

Would you rather really good looking but dumb, or ugly but very smart?

Would you rather have a very large nose or freakishly small eyes?

Would you rather have friends that are much better looking than you or way smarter than you?

Would you rather be the best player on a losing team or the worst player on a winning team?

Would you rather listen to music all day everyday or not listen at all?

Would you rather give up your phone for 2 weeks or your computer for 1 month?

Would you rather help your crush pass and exam or your best friend?

Would you rather have a cough that didn't go away or a hiccup that didn't go away?

Would you rather delete Snapchat or stop watching Instagram stories?

Would you rather get a really bad gift for Christmas or no gifts at all?

Would you rather cheat on a test or fail a test?

Would you rather have an adopted sibling or find out you were adopted?

Would you rather have a weird smile or a weird laugh?

Would you rather have a monkey that talk or dances?

Would you rather have tentacles for hands or legs?

Would you rather always laugh at sad things or always cry at funny things?

Would you rather have wings but can't fly or a tail?

Would you rather use someone else's tooth brush or find out someone else used yours?

Would you rather wear oversized clothes to school or clothes that were too tight?

Would you rather have a childish older sibling or a younger one who bosses you around?

Would you rather eat a bar of soap or drink liquid soap?

Would you rather have dandruff in your hair or not shower for 1 month?

Would you rather have a wide face or a long face?

Would you rather be alone when you're sick or lots of friends around?

Would you rather win a motorcycle or a hover board?

Would you rather use an iPhone or Samsung?

Would you rather have a maid or a chef?

Would you rather work part time in a bookstore or in a clothing store?

Would you rather watch a reality show or be in one?

Would you rather go fishing or hunting?

Would you rather have a best friend who's an introvert or an extrovert?

Would you rather get a follow on Instagram from Barack Obama or Kim Kardashian?

Would you rather dress fashionably or comfortably?

Would you rather be chased by a hobo or a hobo's dog?

Would you rather have a friend that smells weird or acts weird?

Would you rather laugh so hard you started crying or laugh so hard you couldn't breathe?

Would you rather have a gap between your two front teeth or braces?

Would you rather be so tired your mom had to bathe you or your best friend had to bathe you?

Would you rather fall into a swimming pool or into a puddle of water?

Would you rather have parents that looked unusually young or have parents that dressed like young people?

Would you rather be the class clown or the school mascot?

Would you rather have elf ears or really long fingers?

Would you rather have permanent locks for your hair or be permanently bald?

Would you rather always know where you future kids are or always know where your future spouse is?

Would you rather be 18 forever or 30 forever?

Would you rather have a French accent or an Australian accent?

Would you rather have siblings who drive you crazy or be an only child and be lonely?

Would you rather all your friends hang out at your place or you all go somewhere like the mall?

Would you rather have a locker at school that was a time machine or one that brought you to an alternate reality?

Would you rather be able to see into the future or read minds?

Would you rather perform a dance in a talent show or sing a song?

Would you rather tell your friend a white lie or tell the truth that you know will hurt them but was necessary?

Would you rather wash your mouth with pepper or soap?

Would you rather work at an animal shelter or an internet café?

Would you rather eliminate basketball as a sport or hockey?

Would you rather dress like a clown for the rest of your life or become half your height?

Would you rather lose your privacy from becoming famous or lose your friends?

Would you rather believe that aliens exist or that animals could speak?

Would you rather invest the telephone if you went back in time or the television?

Would you rather snort anytime you laugh or snore extremely loud every time you sleep?

Would you rather change your past or be in control of your future?

Would you rather eat a large bar of butter or a bottle of vinegar?

Would you rather have a talking dog or talking cat?

Would you rather bowl all day or skate all day?

Would you rather master the violin or guitar?

Would you rather open your own restaurant or get a high paying finance job later in life?

Would you rather look like Donald trump or act like Donald trump?

Would you rather switch bodies with your mom or dad?

Would you rather switch heads with the person on your left or on your right?

Would you rather accidently walk into a glass wall or brick wall?

Would you rather sound like a chicken when you laugh or like a duck?

Would you rather go back to being a baby or fast forward to being 50?

Would you rather slap a seal or get slapped by a seal?

Would you rather drink your own snot or blood?

Would you rather become your sibling for 1 day or have your sibling become your twin?

Would you rather be only able to send text messages or receive them?

Would you rather have no phone after 7pm or have complete computer monitoring by your parents?

Would you rather get your first kiss in front of your school or in front of your family?

Would you rather work as a clown your whole life to be homeless for 6 months?

Would you rather have a swimming pool or a Jacuzzi?

Would you rather write a popular book or direct a popular movie?

Would you rather have bad breath or bad body odor?

Would you rather be emotionless or feel things too much?

Would you rather live life as an entrepreneur with the stresses or be stuck at a job with decent pay your whole life?

Would you rather be in great shape but never eat junk food or eat bad and look normal?

Would you rather live without YouTube or Instagram?

Would you rather be overweight or be really hairy?

Would you rather snort a teaspoon of cinnamon or be sick in bed for 1 week?

Would you rather have 3 nipples or 1 nipple?

Would you rather find love that lasts forever or cure cancer?

Would you rather listen to rap music for the rest of your life or country music?

Would you rather your parents be together but hate each other or be divorced and very happy?

Would you rather pet a gorilla or a lion, assuming they're both dangerous?

Would you rather starve to death or eat human forever?

Would you rather be burned alive or freeze to death?

Would you rather stub your toe or get a paper cut?

Would you rather go skydiving or scuba diving?

Would you rather be the best looking of your friends or the richest?

Would you rather have a personal chef or a personal masseuse?

Would you rather have sensitive smell or sensitive hearing?

Would you rather eat mac and cheese for the rest of your life of chicken nuggets?

Would you rather become a doctor or a pilot?

Would you rather make a child cry or kick a puppy?

Would you rather be gossiped about or be lied to?

Would you rather get shot out of a canon on walk across a high wire?

Would you rather eat a whole pack of Oreos or a bottle of Pringles?

Would you rather be a fast writer or a fast reader?

Would you rather go to a picnic or a cookout?

Would you rather spend the holidays at your grandma's or at your cousin's?

Would you rather watch a comedy movie or a horror movie?

Would you rather eat something grilled or something roasted?

Would you rather be able to make the best paste ever or be able to flip eggs perfectly while cooking them?

Would you rather have a big bed but small room or small bed but a big room?

Would you rather have blue eyes or green eyes?

Would you rather only eat vegetables for 1 week or just apples for 1 week?

Would you rather make a lot of money or be good looking?

Would you rather get sent to military school or scoop dog poop at a dog park for 2 weeks?

Would you rather win $100 gift card to somewhere you don't like or get $200 cash?

Printed in Great Britain
by Amazon